pastor

FRED OAKS

BUILDING A PRODUCTIVE
PASTOR–CONGREGATION PARTNERSHIP
IN 40 DAYS.

FaithWalk
PUBLISHING
Grand Haven, Michigan

Printed in the United States of America
10 09 08 07 06 05   7 6 5 4 3 2 1

        Library of Congress Cataloging-in-Publication Data

Oaks, Fred.
  Welcome, pastor! : building a productive pastor/congregation partnership in 40 days / by Fred Oaks.—1st ed.
     p. cm.
  ISBN-13: 978-1-932902-50-1 (pbk. : alk. paper)
  ISBN-10: 1-932902-50-3
  1. Pastoral theology. I. Title.
  BV4011.3.O25 2005
  253'.2--dc22
                  2005014888

DEDICATION

*To Judy with gratitude for our partnership
in Christian marriage.*

CONTENTS

Explanation of the 40-Day Process

Building the Foundation

Supplemental Material

ACKNOWLEDGMENTS

Thanks to Mark Shaw of Books for Life Foundation, who inspired me; to Brent Bill of the Indianapolis Center for Congregations, who encouraged me; to literary agent William Brown, who guided me; and to publisher Dirk Wierenga of FaithWalk, whose passion for books that assist readers on spiritual journeys is contagious. It is a joy to share the journey with you all.

EXPLANATION OF THE 40-DAY PROCESS

A lighthouse is built to last. Every detail of construction is meaningful. The location of the lighthouse, the design of the structure, and the building materials are all carefully chosen. Shortcuts are not taken, shoddy workmanship is not tolerated, and nothing is left to chance.

This level of detail is necessary because a lighthouse must stand against opposition like no other structure in the world. Wind and sea assault it continuously. Fierce storms hurl their fury against it with incredible force. Yet a well made lighthouse endures. In any weather, it guides passing ships and warns them away from the rocks that would sink them.

The strength of its foundation determines whether a lighthouse remains in place year after year. Even the brightest beacon in the sturdiest tower is useless unless it is secured to a strong base. The foundation transmits the load of the tower to the supporting rock. It prevents slippage even when wind and sea do their worst. As long as the foundation holds, the beacon will shine. If it fails, the tower topples, its light swallowed by dark, menacing waves.

The world's most famous lighthouse is renowned for its foundation. Smeaton's Eddystone Lighthouse can still be seen today in Plymouth, England, nearly 250 years after its construction. Great care was taken to secure the granite tower to the underlying rock. Foundation stones of the lower courses were dovetailed and set into corresponding dovetails cut into the rock. For higher courses, the stones were carefully interlocked and pinned to the levels above and below. All this took two years of work under difficult conditions in a stormy sea channel, but the resulting structure was extremely secure. Designed by John Smeaton and first lit in 1759, it withstood the battering of the sea for more than 100 years, and is still recognized as one of the greatest engineering feats of all time.

Like John Smeaton, you have an opportunity to build something that endures. Your work will help people in ways you will not fully know on this side of eternity. You are building a pastor–congregation partnership, and this book will help you construct it successfully.

The way you start sets a pattern you'll keep for a long time, for better or worse. After working with congregations for many years, Kennon Callahan warned new pastors: "Your first three days shape the first three weeks. You can never make a first impression the second time. The first three weeks shape the first three months. How you as pastor use this time together with your congregation shapes the first three years. How you begin shapes how you continue and where you end."[1]

In other words, how you *start up* determines where you *end up*. If you invest in building a strong partnership now, you will enjoy a relationship of fruitful cooperation for years.

Point of Beginning

Surveyors use the term "point of beginning" to designate the starting point of a survey. As you begin to build your pastor–congregation partnership, it is helpful to note your point of beginning. Two things deserve attention: First, has the new pastor been called or appointed? Second, what was the quality of the congregation's relationship with the new pastor's predecessor?

Pastors are usually called or appointed. In some traditions, congregations call their pastors. When a pastoral vacancy occurs, a pulpit or search committee is selected to begin a search. This group solicits applications, screens interested persons, conducts interviews, and selects a candidate to recommend to the church. The church then decides whether to call that candidate to the position of pastor. In other traditions, a church authority assigns pastors to congregations for a specified period of service. Sometimes these appointments must be ratified by the congregation. Whether the match is made by the congregation or a church authority, the 40-day process described in this book fosters a relationship between pastor and people that is intimate, vital, and sacred.

A significant influence on your point of beginning is the congregation's relationship with the new pastor's predecessor. Depending on the circumstances, the departure of the predecessor may have evoked feelings ranging from despair to delight. For example, a dearly loved pastor who retires after twenty-five years of faithful service will inspire feelings of loss and grief among most members. On the other hand, a pastor who resigns under pressure after eighteen painful months will likely leave many parishioners feeling relieved. These are extreme examples; in most cases, a departing pastor has strengths that are appreciated and weaknesses that cause concern. When that person leaves, church members will feel grateful for the departing pastor's service and enthused about the opportunities available to the pastor's successor.

What is your point of beginning as you start building this pastor–congregation partnership? How does that influence your willingness to invest time and energy in this process?

Start as Jesus Did

Jesus started with prayer. After he was baptized, the Spirit led him into the wilderness, where he remained for forty days (Mt 4:1–11). Forty days of prayer and reflection are a wonderful way to begin shared ministry. After all, what results can you expect if you rush into the *tasks* of ministry without building *relationships* with God and one another? Adrenaline is a poor substitute for the leading of the Holy Spirit. God has brought you together as pastor and people to serve the Lord's purpose. When you begin with a season of prayer, you imitate his example.

Jesus declared to his followers, "You are the light of the world" (Mt 5:14). Your church is a spiritual lighthouse. It offers direction and hope to people. It guides and warns. It will continue to banish the darkness, despite daily erosion and occasional storms, if it is attached to a secure foundation. Use this book to build that foundation through prayer, Bible study, and dialogue. Strengthen the bonds that make serving Jesus together a joy. Start by building love, trust, and mutual respect.

You've been called to a work site. You're entering a construction zone. During the next forty days, you will develop the partnership between pastor and congregation. It is the foundation for ministry, a foundation affixed to the underlying rock of Almighty God. "For who is God except the Lord? Who but our God is a solid rock?" (Ps 18:31).

How to Use this Book

Just as interlocking stones connect the foundation blocks of a lighthouse and anchor them to the underlying rock, so will using this book strengthen the pastor–congregation partnership and secure it to God. You will build strength gradually, day by day, through prayer and conversation. Beginning at a time you choose and continuing for forty days, you commit to two things: devotions and dialogue.

Devotions

The devotions in *Welcome, Pastor!* have been written specifically for a congregation welcoming a new pastor, associate pastor, or ministry program specialist. They shine the light of God's Word on the four core challenges of any successful start-up:

1. **Getting to know one another** by sharing love and laughter, hurts and hopes
2. **Sharing faith** honestly and authentically
3. **Discerning what God expects** of us as pastor and people
4. **Speaking openly about differences** in order to handle them constructively

During start-up, you address all of these challenges at the same time. All four are woven throughout the book. Mastering one improves your ability to master all the others.

This mastery comes at a price. You should read and reflect for at least fifteen minutes each day. When and where are up to you. Some people find that using the same time and place works best for them. Others prefer a more flexible approach. Whenever and wherever you have your quiet time, begin by asking God's Spirit to guide you. Then read and reflect on the day's Scripture passage, followed by the devotion. Pray for insight. Pray for others. Pray for yourself. Then make a brief entry in your journal.

If this is your first experience with journaling, relax and enjoy it. Do not be concerned about length, spelling, punctuation, or grammar. They aren't the important parts. No one will know what you have written unless you choose to share it. The important thing is to write something each day. The writing becomes a record of your reflections and gives you something to share with others, if you choose, during dialogue meetings.

Dialogue

Every ten days—four times in all—you will meet with others in your church who are participating in this process. The speaking and listening in these meetings, coupled with the power of prayer, develop a strong pastor-congregation partnership. The supplemental material (pp. 99–102) will help you prepare for these important meetings.

Getting Started

Are you ready to begin? Commit yourself to this work. Then recruit additional people to join you. Other tasks may seem more *urgent*, but none is more *important* than building this foundation with God's help. If you are the new pastor or ministry leader, invite the people of your congregation to join you in this process. If you are a layperson, speak with your new pastor about it. In either case, your message is simple: *"This start-up phase is vital to our future. Will you join me in forty days of devotions and dialogue to build a strong foundation for partnership?"*

The people who accept this invitation are your group. Include as many people as you like. The entire congregation can use this book to bathe start-up in prayer. It can also be used by a pastoral search committee, a pastor–parish relations committee, an adult Sunday School class, a Bible Study group, or a prayer cell. The number of people willing to participate may surprise you.

Introductory Meeting

Welcome, Pastor! helps you set the tone for your new pastor–congregation partnership. In the same way, an introductory meeting can set the tone for your *Welcome, Pastor!* usage. Here's how:

1. Choose the beginning and ending dates of your forty days of prayer and dialogue.

2. Communicate the dates to potential participants well in advance. Use your newsletter, announcements, website, worship bulletins, and prayer groups. Here is a sample message: **Welcome, Pastor! Group Forming—**Help create a positive partnership with our new pastor! Pastor (name) and (sponsoring group) invite you to participate in the *Welcome, Pastor!* process. All you need is a Bible and a copy of *Welcome, Pastor! Building a Productive Pastor–Congregation Partnership in 40 Days.* This devotional book is especially helpful to churches with new pastors. We'll begin (starting date) and conclude (ending date). Please attend a no-obligation introductory meeting (time, place). For more information contact (name, phone #, e-mail address). Through prayer and dialogue, we will form a partnership that starts strong and endures."

3. At the introductory meeting, tell people about the daily devotional time. Invite someone who prays faithfully to describe briefly why they make time for daily Scripture reading and prayer. Be sensitive to those who have never established such a habit. Next,

tell the group about the four core challenges of starting up and the four dialogue meetings. Have a supply of *Welcome, Pastor!* books on hand. In each book, place a bookmark listing starting and ending dates as well as the dates and locations of the dialogue meetings.

4. Ask, "What benefits might God bring to our church through the *Welcome, Pastor!* process?" List responses on flipchart or an overhead projector.

5. Finally, provide time for people to decide whether they will commit to the forty days of the *Welcome, Pastor!* process. Those who choose to participate should sign the covenant on page 10.

6. Conclude the meeting with a prayer for the success of your *Welcome, Pastor!* process.

Group Covenant

Commit to building a fruitful relationship by signing this covenant:

"With God's help, I commit to building a strong foundation for the pastor–congregation partnership forming in our church, throughout the next forty days.

1. I will read the Bible and *Welcome, Pastor!* daily.
2. I will pray regularly for the pastor and all other participants.
3. I will keep a journal of brief written reflections.
4. Barring an emergency, I will participate in the four dialogue meetings held at 10-day intervals.

Signature: _____

Date: _____

You are building the foundation of a spiritual lighthouse. Give it your best.

BUILDING THE FOUNDATION

Day 1
"Who's There?"

Scripture Reading: Luke 4:1–13

Key Verse:
> *"Then Jesus, full of the Holy Spirit, left the Jordan River. He was led by the Spirit to go out into the wilderness, where the Devil tempted him for forty days."*
> —Luke 4:1–2a

"Knock, knock!"

"Who's there?"

When a congregation welcomes a new pastor, both are asking the question, "Who's there?" Each wonders: "What are you like? What experiences have made you who you are? What is important to you? What hopes do you cherish? Where will we go together? What will our relationship become?"

You will invest in relationships for these forty days. You will spend time with God in prayer. You will converse with others in dialogue meetings. Gradually, your knowledge of God and others will grow. Bonds will form. You will build the foundation of a spiritual lighthouse.

Jesus himself began with forty days of prayer. Like Israel before him (Nm 14:33), he was led into the wilderness to undergo a time of testing. In contrast to the unfaithfulness of the Israelites, Jesus remained faithful. Testing in the wilderness prepared him for service in the towns and villages.

Each time the Tempter made Jesus an offer, he was asking, "Who's there?" And each time Jesus refused a temptation, he made answer. Resisting temptation can prepare you for new avenues of service. After the testing, Jesus called followers and taught them.

These forty days of prayer and dialogue offer a wonderful opportunity to ask and answer the question, "Who's there?" During this time, with God's help, you will form a partnership between pastor and congregation marked by love, trust, and mutual respect. Commit to pray, reflect, and journal each day. Participate in the four dialogue meetings. The investment will allow your spiritual lighthouse to shine through many seasons of ministry. Clear identity produces definite purpose. When you know who you are, you know what to do.

Journal

Do you recall a time of testing that revealed who you were and prepared you for a new avenue of service? Write briefly about it.

Day 2
"A Question"

Scripture Reading: Mark 10:46–52

Key Verse:
"What do you want me to do for you?" Jesus asked.
—Mark 10:51

Jesus asked questions. Religious authorities usually make speeches and issue statements. But Jesus often asked questions of the people he met.

One of them was a poor blind beggar named Bartimaeus. Bartimaeus had been sitting by the roadside on the outskirts of Jericho, probably for a long time. He had been blind even longer. Have you ever seen crowds of people pass beggars on city streets? If so, it will be easy for you to imagine the crowd in Jericho brushing past Bartimaeus without notice. But Bartimaeus noticed the crowd! Seizing the opportunity, he called out to Jesus.

Jesus had Bartimaeus summoned and addressed him with a question: "What do you want me to do for you?" (Mk 10:51). Bartimaeus did not hesitate. He knew.

Imagine Jesus addressing the same question to you today. *What do you want me to do for you?* What are your needs as you begin this new pastor–congregation partnership? What are the needs of your congregation? What things create a positive, productive working relationship? What is your role in creating that relationship, and what is the role of the Holy Spirit?

Perhaps sometimes you work so hard to appear capable and self-sufficient that you fail to ask the Lord for help. That is regrettable, for he is eager to assist. He encourages you to ask in his name for what you need and assures you that you will receive (Jn 16:24).

Bartimaeus jumped up when Jesus sent for him (Mk 10:50). When you recognize your spiritual poverty, you will become as keen as he was to bring your requests to the Lord. What do you want Jesus to do for you?

Journal

What words or phrases describe a positive, productive partnership between pastor and congregation? Jot them down. If a symbol or word picture comes to mind, sketch it. Then ask Jesus in prayer for what you want.

Day 3
"The Gift of Pastors"

Scripture Reading: Ephesians 4:1–16

Key Verse:
"He is the one who gave these gifts to the church: ... pastors ..."
—Ephesians 4:11

God has gifted every member of the church to serve all the others. Each Christian has a specific role to play. When we use our gifts for the common good, the church is built up and strengthened. Unfortunately, Christians who do not know their spiritual gifts cannot use them.

That is one way pastors strengthen the church. Pastors help Christians discover talents that have been hidden and therefore unused. This is similar to truffle hunting. In southern France, truffles are cultivated. They are not chocolate; they are hard, plum-sized balls of black fungus that grow underground. Truffles are extremely valuable because they are rare. Chefs worldwide prize the shavings for the intoxicating earthy aroma they add to gourmet dishes.

Some French truffle hunters with well trained noses can detect a truffle hidden up to a foot under ground. (Dogs with this ability fetch prices in the tens of thousands of dollars.) Good pastors perform a similar function. They discover hidden treasures—the gifts of God's people—that can then be lifted up, celebrated, and used for the benefit of others to the glory of God.

When we realize that everyone in the church has been called to service by virtue of their baptism, we recognize immediately the value of pastors. Pastors are the people God has chosen to train Christians in the discovery and use of their gifts. When this training is effective, God's people mature spiritually and the whole church becomes stronger, because the whole body is fitted together perfectly. As each part does its own special work, it helps the other parts grow, so that the whole body is healthy and growing and full of love (Eph 4:16). In this way a pastor's service builds up the church, the body of Christ, and brings people closer to maturity in Christ, who is the head.

Journal

Write about a time when a pastor or ministry leader helped you discover a gift or special ability. If you have not yet had this experience, write briefly about a gift or talent you think God may have given you.

Day 4
"Rumblings"

Scripture Reading: Acts 6:1–6

Key Verse:
> " ... *there were rumblings of discontent.* "
>
> —Acts 6:1

In 1974 Charlton Heston starred in the movie *Earthquake*. It was a disaster epic that centered on a devastating Los Angeles earthquake and its shocking aftermath. The film was shown in theaters with a sound process known as "Sensurround." This process caused cinemas to physically vibrate during quake sequences. *Earthquake* was nominated for four Academy Awards, and won one for—you guessed it—best sound.

Most churches have their own version of "Sensurround." When a church seems to be sliding into decline, there are rumblings. There are rumblings when a church grows, too, because changes are taking place. Discontented church people find ways to make known their displeasure. These rumblings send tremors through a fellowship.

In Acts 6, the rumblings of discontent were grounded in differences in culture and amplified by differences in language. The church, growing rapidly, had a problem. Leaders responded with a creative solution. Note the pattern: rumblings, response, and innovation.

Rumblings of discontent may shake the church, but they are valuable. We may want our congregation to be hassle-free, a peaceful refuge from all conflict. But if there are no differences in a fellowship, energy for growth and change is lost.

Some conflict in a congregation is normal, even necessary. It is an invitation to learn.

Throughout the history of the church, rumblings have stimulated creativity. When Christian leaders respond to conflicts in a sensitive and timely manner, the church makes progress.

Journal

Has there been a time when the pattern "rumblings, response, innovation" has played out in your congregation? Briefly describe it.

Day 5
"First Impressions"

Scripture Reading: John 1:35–51

Key Verse:
Looking intently at Simon, Jesus said, "You are Simon, the son of John—but you will be called Cephas (which means Peter)."
—John 1:42

Attending class on the first day of school. Stepping into the room for a job interview. Meeting a prospective client for a business lunch. Visiting a new church. In these and many other situations, we make and take first impressions.

With only limited information, we make inferences and draw conclusions about others. They do the same. Sometimes these conclusions are accurate. Other times they are wildly mistaken. But there is undisputed power in a first impression, and we get only one shot.

Simon, the son of John, certainly made an impression on Jesus. Jesus studied the man and then declared, "'You will be called Cephas' (which means Peter)" (Jn 1:42). Cephas and Peter both mean "rock." Apparently, Peter gave an impression of strength and durability. His confession of Christ became the foundation of the Church (Mt 16:16-18).

What kind of impression do you make? Have you ever been given a nickname as the result of a first impression? Ever assigned a handle to someone else? Do you know of a person who carried a nickname around for years after a hasty judgment resulted in a memorable moniker?

When a new pastor arrives, both the pastor and congregation make and take first impressions. The first worship service, the first personal interaction, and the first group meeting all produce first impressions. Throughout the initial days and weeks of this new relationship, be aware that you are making and taking first impressions.

The best way to make a good first impression is to forget yourself and become genuinely interested in others. Paul wrote in Philippians 2:3–4, "Don't be selfish; don't live to make a good impression on others. Be humble, thinking of others as better than yourself. Don't think only about your own affairs, but be interested in others, too, and what they are doing." Anyone who heeds that wisdom will make the best possible first impression.

Journal

When you make a first impression, what do you want people to remember about you? Write down three or four adjectives that describe the impression you wish to make.

Day 6
"In God's Presence"

Scripture Reading: Psalm 16:1–11

Key Verse:
"You will show me the way of life, granting me the joy of your
presence and the pleasures of living with you forever."
                                            —Psalm 16:11

How different is a picture of the ocean from the real thing!
Gaze at a photograph of Daytona Beach, and you get a visual
image of sand and water. Visit the same place in person, however, and you have a very different experience. Moist, warm
sand oozes between your toes. A breeze plays in your hair.
Your ears are filled with the rhythmic rolling of waves that
swell and fade, swell and fade. The shrieks of seagulls pierce
the air. On the horizon, water sparkles and glistens in the
sun under an azure sky. Wind-swelled, a rainbow-colored sail
propels a boat across the surface. Step closer to the water and
mist sprays your face, tasting of salt.

Keep the photograph. I'll opt for the visit anytime.

Isn't the presence of God like that? Others may try to describe God, attempt to convey something of their experience
of God. But such descriptions are hardly worth comparing to
experiencing God's presence firsthand. Music and art must
pick up where language leaves off. The psalmist exudes, "No
wonder my heart is filled with joy, and my mouth shouts his
praises!" (Ps 16:9).

Your experience of the Holy Spirit provides a foretaste of
the glory you will share in eternity (Rom 8:23). Like a din-

ner guest sampling delicious appetizers before a feast, you are filled with anticipation. It is wonderful, yes, but there is much more to come!

Journal

Write about a time when you experienced God's presence. How did it feel?

Day 7
"The Power of Focus"

Scripture Reading: Philippians 3:12–16

Key Verse:
"I am focusing all my energies on this one thing…"
—Philippians 3:13

Light can be scattered or focused. The light you read by is scattered. A 100-watt light bulb in a table lamp spreads soft light equally in all directions. A laser beam, on the other hand, focuses light. Lasers apply energy quickly to very small areas. Laser technology is used to etch glass, sterilize wine, vaporize tumors, seal blood vessels, clear blockages in arteries, measure distances, guide missiles, and read compact disks. Communications links use coded light pulses from lasers traveling in glass fibers. A single 144-fiber cable can carry 40,000 telephone conversations in the same instant! Lasers are useful because they are focused.

Like light, the energy of your life can be either scattered or focused. God has entrusted you with time and energy. How will you use them? Will you ask God to show you how best to invest the precious days, hours, and minutes of your life?

People who focus discover great power. They invest time and energy strategically, and so produce results. The Apostle Paul worked toward that day when he would finally be all that Christ Jesus had saved him for and wanted him to be (Phil 3:12). That is a clear and compelling goal. Paul knew what he wanted to achieve. He did not say, "I am dabbling in these twenty things," but "I am focusing all my energies on this one thing" (Phil 3:13). There is power in focus, as Paul's extraordinary life attests. That is true of individual Christians, and it is true of congregations.

Journal

Do you personally have a clear, compelling goal that determines how you invest your time and energy? Does your congregation?

Day 8
"The Value of Struggle"

Scripture Reading: Romans 5:1–5

Key Verse:
"We can rejoice, too, when we run into problems and trials,
for we know that they are good for us…"
—Romans 5:3

When she retired, a woman planted butterfly bushes in her backyard. Now their white, yellow, and lavender flowers perfume the breeze and attract even more colorful butterflies. The woman is dazzled by them. On lazy summer afternoons she sips lemonade on her patio, drinks in the sunshine, and watches butterflies. They come careening along in crazy zigzag flight patterns to land upon the blooms.

Did you know that butterflies would be unable to fly were it not for the struggle of freeing themselves from their cocoons? That is the final stage in their remarkable development. In the larva stage, they are caterpillars that feed and grow. Next comes the pupa, which may be inside a hard shell or enclosed in a cocoon. While there, a change takes place. An adult forms.

When fully formed, the adult breaks out of the pupal shell or cocoon and works to climb free. Once free, its outer structures harden. Its wings, at first small pads, expand greatly, flatten out, and become firm. Eventually, a breeze catches it up and it takes flight! Anyone who tries to "help" a butterfly out of its pupal shell actually dooms it. The struggle to free itself gives the creature the strength it needs for the next stage of life.

Give thanks for struggles. Problems and trials produce strength. Congregations who endure tough times emerge stronger in important ways. Pastors and church leaders who guide a church through adversity often look back with gratitude. They see in retrospect that God used the trials to impart strength—strength the church needed for its next stage of development.

Journal

Describe one way that problems or trials have strengthened your life or congregation.

Day 9
"Transitions"

Scripture Reading: Acts 20:36–38

Key Verse:
> *"Sad most of all because he had said that they*
> *would never see him again."*
> —Acts 20:38a

Have you noticed that prayer and tears often flow together? Prayer comes from the deepest part of us. The feelings underlying our prayers are often very strong. Sometimes they are so strong that words fail, and we trust the Holy Spirit to intercede for us (Rom 8:26).

When we pray with other Christians we form durable bonds. We may soon forget people we've chatted with, but those with whom we have prayed, we remember. The Book of Acts records many impromptu prayer meetings. Paul's farewell to the elders of Ephesus is a powerful example. Just five verses later we find another example of a similar prayer meeting—this one involving believers of all ages (Acts 21:5). In both situations, people were grieving. God brought them together for a time and they shared a season of life and ministry. When that time ended, goodbyes were hard. People wept.

Welcoming a new pastor is a time of beginnings. However, every beginning starts with an ending. Something ends, creating an opportunity for something new to develop. Members of a congregation say goodbye to one pastor before they can welcome another. Pastors and their family members bid farewell to members of the former congregation and community before arriving in the new place to serve the new congregation. The departures and arrivals of pastoral transitions create a bittersweet emotional experience.

Healthy transitions require us to name what we are grieving. Once we have acknowledged the loss, we can mourn appropriately. What are you losing? Who are you leaving behind? Sharing the story of these losses can be an important way to bond with those in our new situation. Talking honestly with one another about our losses connects us. It frees us to embrace the opportunities afforded to us by our new situation.

Journal

What endings are you grieving at this time in your life? With whom might you share this grief?

Day 10
"Thankful"

Scripture Reading: Philippians 1:1–11

Key Verse:
> *"Every time I think of you, I give thanks to my God."*
> —Philippians 1:3

Some people are a joy to know because they are so complimentary. They see our best qualities. They point out our most positive characteristics to us and to others. They build our confidence and self-esteem. It's not just that they flatter. Rather, they simply appreciate desirable traits in the people around them. And there are many people around them, because everyone enjoys their company.

Someone observed that two-thirds of what we see is behind our eyes. If we look for faults, flaws, and problems, we will spot them everywhere in abundance. But if we watch for virtue, excellence, and goodness, then we will perceive those things.

The Apostle Paul looked for positive qualities and encouraged others to do the same (Phil 4:8). He traveled widely and cultivated relationships with a variety of different churches. Each time he wrote to one of them, Paul began the missive with appreciation. (Galatians is the sole exception. Paul's grave concern about their misunderstanding of the gospel compelled him to forego thanksgiving.) Paul enjoyed strong rapport with the believers in Philippi. He remembered their prayers, financial support, and hospitality with deep gratitude.

What are the praiseworthy traits of your congregation? What are the areas of excellence? What is there about your church that is right and lovely and admirable? Your church is unique among the 350,000 congregations in America. Celebrate what is commendable about it by offering thanks to God.

Journal

List a few of your church's best qualities. What are your strengths as a congregation? Thank God for them in prayer.

Dialogue Meeting 1

For ten days you have invited God to speak to you through Scripture, prayer, and journaling. Now you will meet with others in your church who have been praying, too. At times you will learn from them, and at other times you will be their teacher. To get the most out of this meeting, please read the brief section at the back of the book entitled, "About Dialogue Meetings."

A good verse to keep in mind during this first dialogue meeting is 1 Thessalonians 5:14. *"Brothers and sisters, we urge you to warn those who are lazy. Encourage those who are timid. Take tender care of those who are weak. Be patient with everyone."* Some group members may have failed to follow through on their commitment to pray daily. They may have neglected to make it a priority. Warn them lovingly. Some group members may be timid about sharing what God is teaching them during their prayer time. Encourage them when they do speak, and thank them for their contributions. Some may be spiritually weak, struggling with personal problems; care for them. Be patient and understanding with everyone. Trust God to use each one to strengthen the pastor–congregation partnership.

Dialogue Starters

1. Have you sensed that God has spoken to you in the past ten days? If so, in what way(s)?

2. What are you learning about the pastor–congregation partnership that is currently under construction?

3. What ideas or insights from your devotional time during the past ten days have been especially meaningful to you?

4. Finish this sentence: "For me, this first 10-day period of devotions has been like … "

5. How would you like the group to pray *for you* during the next ten days? Be specific.

After this meeting, you will be better acquainted with other members of your group. You will know specifically how to pray for each one. You are becoming a team. Your shared effort to build a productive pastor–congregation partnership is under way!

Day 11
"Pace"

Scripture Reading: Hebrews 12:1–12

Key Verse:
"And let us run with endurance the race that God has set before us."
—Hebrews 12:1

Distance runners know that pace is crucial. If they start out too fast, they become exhausted late in the race and can't finish well. If they wait too long to hit stride, they squander an opportunity for a strong showing. Runners practice daily to establish optimum pace. They study the racecourse to learn its unique features. On race day, staying on pace is their key to success.

We Christians run in the greatest race of all—a race set before us by God. We run it with other believers in the church. To run with endurance requires us to pace ourselves for the long haul. We set pace by discerning what changes God would have us make, then sensitively making them.

There are two basic kinds of changes. First, there are those thrust upon us by forces outside our congregation. These changes are beyond our control, but we must respond to them as best we can. Second, there are the changes we introduce to achieve a desired result. Sometimes we change to remain relevant in a changing world. At other times, we change in hopes of becoming more faithful or effective.

It is important that we are able to talk with one another about what we feel should change and what should not. We should also communicate with one another about the pace of change. Managing change is one of the most challenging and rewarding activities in the life of any congregation.

Change is certain—and out of our control. We can, however, choose our responses to external changes and manage the pace of the changes that we introduce. Pushing for too much too fast can create resentment and anger. Failing to act in a timely manner can mean forfeiting precious opportunities. Pace is crucial.

Journal

Write or sketch a word, phrase, or picture that describes the pace of change in your congregation. Do you feel that the pace of change in recent times has been too fast, too slow, or about right? What change might occur in your church to create greater openness to God's leading?

Day 12
"Strength in Diversity"

Scripture Reading: 1 Corinthians 12:4–27

Key Verse:
> *"A spiritual gift is given to each of us*
> *as a means of helping the entire church."*
> —1 Corinthians 12:7

Certain species of birds are dependent on hippos. Aquatic birds such as herons and egrets perch on the backs of hippos to catch fish. Oxpeckers gobble up ticks and leeches that attach themselves to the hippos' sides. The oxpeckers also clean out wounds and trim away dead skin from the hippos. For their part, hippos excrete vital nutrients to rivers and lakes every day. These nutrients help maintain an adequate stock of fish. The birds, hippos, and fish are all connected in a dynamic circle of life.

God has created a world in which living things depend upon each other. Delicate ecosystems in forest, field, and stream illustrate this mutual interdependence. We are all connected in a great web of life.

God's new creation, the Church, likewise thrives on diversity. The Church teaches each of its members to value and appreciate those who are different. This is God's design. The Church is composed of individual Christians, and every one has received at least one spiritual gift (1 Pt 4:10). We who belong to one another in the Church are to use our gifts to serve others. When we do, we build up the congregation. Our particular strengths contrast with and complement the strengths of others. They, in turn, serve us with their strengths.

Hands, feet, ears, and eyes perform very different functions. Yet the body needs each of them to achieve top performance. When each part is performing its role in harmony with the others, differences actually create a stronger whole. In the Church, Christians serving one another with radically different gifts create a dynamic, healthy congregation. There is strength in diversity when combined with an attitude of service.

Journal

Consider someone in your congregation who is very different from you. How is God using that person to help your church become strong and mature? Write a brief prayer of thanks to God for that person and for the differing gifts evident in your congregation. If you like, sketch a "body" illustrating the strengths and gifts of your church. What are your strengths? Where is greater balance needed?

Day 13
"Sanctuary"

Scripture Reading: Luke 5:12–16

Key Verse:
> *"Jesus often withdrew to the wilderness for prayer."*
> —Luke 5:16

Time out! Every now and then we need to escape the pressures of our daily routines in order to find quiet. Often we allow our schedules to become too full. Energy and creativity are drained away by our customary patterns of relating to people. The demands of home, work, church, and community tax us to exhaustion.

Jesus was widely known for his teaching and healing. Word spread about him; many came to see him, hear him teach, and receive healing. Sometimes the crowds were so vast, Jesus had to make special arrangements simply to speak to all of the people. In the midst of these continual demands, Jesus withdrew. He went away into the wilderness to pray.

Jesus calls us to serve in his name. When we serve in the power of the Holy Spirit, we are effective. We see results, and that energizes us. Serving well often results in new opportunities with greater demands. Unless we are careful, we may find ourselves attempting to serve in our own power instead of God's.

Like Jesus, we must withdraw in order to serve. Do you have a place to which you go when you need to commune with God, listen for God's voice, read, reflect, and meditate? Do you have a special place for prayer? Jesus withdrew to the wilderness; perhaps you also enjoy being outdoors for times of prayer. Or you may have a dedicated space in your home, office, or church for prayer and reflection. Such places often become very significant to us. When we visit them, we can feel ourselves entering into sanctuary.

Where we go is less significant than the fact that we do go away from time to time to pray. It is necessary. We may feel that we are abandoning people as we withdraw from their needs, but it is in order to serve them that we seek solitude to enjoy time with God.

Journal

Are you balancing care of self with care for others? Where do you go for prayer, retreat, and reflection? Write about, draw, or describe a place that has become a sanctuary for you.

Day 14
"The Good Book"

Scripture Reading: 2 Timothy 3:10–17

Key Verse:

> *"All Scripture is inspired by God…"*
> —2 Timothy 3:16

When did you receive your first Bible? What did it look like? If you grew up in church, you probably had one by the time you were old enough to read. If not, you may have been much older. Did those who presented the Bible to you encourage you to adopt a certain attitude toward it?

God's people have always cherished Scripture. The Apostle Paul reminded Timothy that his childhood teachers were trustworthy people who had endured suffering because of their faith. They encouraged Timothy to revere Scripture because it is inspired by God. This unique quality of Scripture gives it the following uses:

First, *it teaches what is true*. In a world of falsehood, deception, and confusion the Bible is a trustworthy source of God's truth.

Second, *it makes us realize what is wrong in our lives*. Scripture can show us things about ourselves we had ignored or overlooked—things that grieve God's heart and prevent us from experiencing fulfillment as Christians.

Third, *it straightens us out*. When we stray from the narrow way and need to be corrected, Scripture restores right thinking and puts our feet on the best path.

Fourth, *it teaches us to do what is right*. This enables us to cultivate habits that produce exceptional character.

Finally, *it equips us to do what God wants us to do.* Studying Scripture is not an end in itself. We study in order to apply. When we apply the truth of Scripture to our lives, we do what God wants us to do. Study promotes obedience.

Journal

What is the role of the Bible in your life? Complete this sentence: "To me, Scripture is like … " Take a few moments to thank God for the gift of Scripture.

Day 15
"Dare to Dream"

Scripture Reading: Eph. 3:14–21

Key Verse:
> *"God … is able to accomplish infinitely more than*
> *we would ever dare to ask or hope."*
>
> —Ephesians 3:20

A fisherman slipped into a rowboat and pushed off from shore to try his luck on a beautiful, pristine lake. It didn't take him long to notice a fly fisherman, hip-deep in water near the shore, pulling in one fish after another. This man's remarkable luck seemed all the more intriguing because he was keeping only small fish and releasing the large ones unharmed.

"Excuse me," called the man in the boat. "I commend you for your skill as a fisherman. Forgive me for asking, but why do you keep only the smaller fish and toss the bigger ones back?"

"Oh, that's easy to explain," replied the fly fisherman. "I have only a small frying pan!"

God's love is beyond our comprehension. We cannot understand it, but we can experience it, and each experience whets our appetite for more. Like God's love, God's power is beyond our ken. Yet that power at work in us, as individuals and as a congregation, is capable of things we have never dared to imagine! How often have we been like the fly fisherman, content with familiar small results when larger ones are ours for the asking? What keeps us from getting a larger 'frying pan' in which to receive a greater measure of God's power to work in us?

Journal

What great dream would you dare to dream for God if you knew you could not fail? What great dream would you dream for your congregation? Write a description of what you or your congregation might be like if you allowed a greater measure of God's power to work in you.

Day 16
"Two Ears"

Scripture Reading: Proverbs 29:20
Key Verse:

> *"There is more hope for a fool*
> *than for someone who speaks without thinking."*
>
> —Proverbs 29:20

Two elderly gentlemen were seated side-by-side on a park bench. One said to the other, "I'd let you talk more, but you're not as interesting as I am." While we would be loath to put it in as many words, we do often feel that way. We are much more interested in ourselves than in our conversation partners. As a result, we are happy to do most of the talking whenever we are together.

This tendency to speak first and listen second (if at all) can prevent us from developing wisdom. The Book of Proverbs offers understanding to those who seek it. One recurring theme is the necessity of good listening coupled with discerning speech. The wise say little and listen much. This attitude gave rise to the observation that the Good Lord gave us two ears and only one mouth to remind us to listen more than we speak. The New Testament carries this theme still further when James observes that taming the tongue is the last frontier of self-control (Jas 3:2).

Good listeners keep a purpose in mind as they listen. They lean forward toward their conversation partner, provide steady eye contact without staring, and give regular feedback that says, "I hear you." This feedback may be nonverbal, like a nod or a sympathetic facial expression. Or it may be verbal, as in,

"Mm-hmm," "Yes, I see," or "Let me see if I understand what you're saying … " followed by a summary statement. The best listeners provide both verbal and nonverbal feedback. They listen for feelings behind words and summarize their conversation partner's thoughts to be sure they have understood them correctly. When they speak, it is to ask a question of the conversation partner, or to build on what that person has already shared.

Good listening is rare because most people would rather talk. But the wise are different, and as a result their wisdom grows.

Journal

Write down the names of people who speak to you frequently. How well have you been listening to them? Today, give them your undivided attention. Summarize what they have shared with you to be sure you have understood correctly. Do not speak until they have finished talking. When you return to this journal, write a brief description of each person's response to your improved listening.

Day 17
"Family"

Scripture Reading: 2 Timothy 1:1–8

Key Verse:
> *"… you have the faith of your mother, Eunice,*
> *and your grandmother, Lois."*
> —2 Timothy 1:5

In some families, Christian faith is of central importance. Scripture is read and discussed openly, family members pray together, weekly worship attendance is a habit, and family members serve others in Jesus's name.

Other families are indifferent about Christian faith. In these homes no Scripture is read aloud, family members do not pray together, worship attendance is rare, and service to others is infrequent.

Still other families are hostile toward Christian faith. In these families, Scripture is attacked as untrustworthy, prayer is mocked, worshipers are dismissed as feeble-minded or hypocritical, and those who serve others are ridiculed.

The Apostle Paul came from a devout family. He tells Timothy that he is serving God just as his ancestors did before him (2 Tm 1:3). Paul says that he is confident that Timothy trusts Jesus Christ, because Timothy shares the faith of his mother and grandmother. He is a third generation Christian.

Our family of origin plays an important role in shaping our understanding of Christ and the church. What faith is, and the importance we should give it, we learn from our family members. Someone observed that Christian faith is more *caught* than *taught*. We catch crucial attitudes and beliefs from parents, siblings, and extended family members.

Journal

What were the attitudes about Christ and the Church held by people in your family of origin? Describe how those attitudes have shaped your own faith.

Day 18
"Good for the Soul"

Scripture Reading: 1 John 1:5–10

Key Verse:

> *"...if we confess our sins to him,*
> *he is faithful and just to forgive us..."*
>
> —1 John 1:9

Shortly after the terrorist attacks of September 11, 2001, a temporary memorial was created at the site of the World Trade Center. Powerful beacons were combined and lit together to create twin towers of light rising from the site of the tragedy. The lights were so powerful they could be seen from space.

John describes a far greater light when teaching about God's perfection and holiness. He declares that God is light and in God there is no darkness at all. Therefore, those who would have fellowship with God—and with those who are living in the light of God's presence—must regularly confess their sins.

The term *sin* originated from the archery range. It means "missing the mark." It described the archers' arrows that strayed from the bull's eye. They were off target or fell short. We may distinguish between sins of commission and sins of omission. Sins of commission are the things we've done that were wrong. Sins of omission are the good things we ought to have done, but failed to do.

Everyone sins. To deny our sins and our need to confess them is to persist in error. We free ourselves from this error and the burden of our guilt when we confess our sins to God.

This allows us to receive God's forgiveness and cleansing. We are pardoned, purified, washed clean. Our relationships with God and other Christians are restored.

Journal

Is confession part of your Christian living? What do you need to confess in order to receive God's forgiveness and cleansing? Thank God for the grace that washes away sin.

Day 19
"Balance"

Scripture Reading: Psalm 23

Key Verse:

> *"He renews my strength."*
>
> —Psalm 23:3

Many of us live at a frantic pace. We rush from one commitment to the next, marking "Things to Do" off of our lists as we complete assigned tasks. We are efficient. We are productive. And at the end of the day we are exhausted. We collapse, feeling spent physically and emotionally. Relaxing is difficult because we expect tomorrow's pace to be the same.

Churches sometimes contribute to this frenzied culture of busy-ness. Church leaders exhort members to invest time and energy in the great cause of extending the reign of God. No organization on earth can enroll people in a more worthy venture. But the church's lofty purposes cannot be served by people too busy to pause.

When we prize activity over reflection, we are out of balance. If we persist, we will attempt to serve God's purposes on our own strength. This always creates a downward spiral: poor results, discouragement, increased effort on our own strength, even poorer results, and so on.

God's way is different. When David wrote Psalm 23, he painted a beautiful picture of resting in lush green meadows and reflecting beside peaceful streams. With his strength thus renewed, David was ready to be guided further along God's path.

In discerning God's best for your pastor–congregation partnership, allow time for contemplation. Healthy churches expect staff and volunteers to make time to pray and reflect regularly. This allows them to serve with renewed strength and a clear sense of God's leading. They are balanced. They are effective. They are not exhausted, but fulfilled.

Right now, spend a few moments simply relaxing in God's presence. Appreciate the beauty of God's good creation. When the right path is revealed, make the journey with all the strength the Lord provides.

Journal

Read the psalm aloud. What words, phrases, or images does the Spirit impress upon you? Jot them down in your journal. Is the pattern of your daily life balanced between activity and reflection? If not, what new opportunities can you create to be renewed for service?

Day 20
"Do It Now"

Scripture Reading: Matthew 5:21–26

Key Verse:

> *"Go and be reconciled to that person."*
> —Matthew 5:24

Go to the dentist. Visit the bureau of motor vehicle registration. Eat a bowl of radishes. There are lots of things we'd rather do than seek to mend a broken relationship, particularly if we feel the other person has made a mountain out of a molehill.

When we become aware that another person has something against us, we have received important information. Sometimes the information comes to us directly from the person; sometimes we get it indirectly. What will we do with it?

Directly addressing a strained relationship is too threatening for many of us to contemplate seriously. We will accept almost any excuse as grounds for avoiding that task. We tell ourselves that the offended person expected too much of us. We find fault with that person or imagine that *they* have done *us* wrong. We assume that our attempts to reconcile would be rebuffed, perhaps even exposing us to personal attack. As a result, we avoid the offended person and excuse our refusal to respond to their pain.

Jesus certainly affirmed the generous giving of God's people (Mk 12:41–44). But in the Sermon on the Mount, he taught his followers to leave their sacrifices at the Temple altar when more pressing business came to mind. Reconciliation is so important, he said, that a worshiper should leave before the benediction to pursue it.

Every congregation consists of sinful people. As a result, there are bound to be hurt feelings and misunderstandings among God's people. When two members are estranged, the strained relationship can affect the entire fellowship. We are to go directly to the person who has something against us, acknowledge their distress, and seek reconciliation. It is the heart of the Gospel (2 Cor 5:19). The beginning of a new pastor–congregation partnership is an ideal time to pursue it.

Journal

Who has something against you? Pray for guidance, then write down a plan with a date by which you will go to that person seeking to be reconciled.

Dialogue Meeting 2

Congratulations! You have reached the mid-point of your 40-day journey. You are following through on your commitment to this process. Others who attend this dialogue meeting are also demonstrating their strong commitment. Give thanks for them! *"Ever since I first heard of your strong faith in the Lord Jesus and your love for Christians everywhere, I have never stopped thanking God for you"* (Eph 1:15-16a). At this meeting, show your respect and thanks to others by being slow to speak and quick to listen.

Dialogue Starters

1. Have you sensed that God has spoken to you in the past ten days? If so, in what way(s)?

2. What are you learning about the pastor–congregation partnership that is currently under construction?

3. What ideas or insights from your devotional time during the past ten days seem especially meaningful to you?

4. Finish this sentence: "For me, this 10-day period of devotions has been like … "

5. How would you like the group to pray for you during the next ten days? Be specific.

By the end of this meeting, you should be well acquainted with your fellow participants. You should be able to count on their prayers and support. The Spirit of God is guiding your group through both private prayer and group dialogue. Your group has started strong; maintain your focus so that you finish well, too.

Day 21
"The Grace of Giving"

Scripture reading: Acts 20:32–35

Key Verse:

> *'It is more blessed to give than to receive.'*
>
> —Acts 20:35

On December 26, 2004, an earthquake under the Indian Ocean sent killer waves, called tsunamis, smashing into coastlines. Tens of thousands of people perished. Devastated communities needed to be rebuilt.

Donations came from people all over the world. Aid flowed in from many sources. One observer compared this outpouring of assistance to the disaster itself. He said, "The waves of water caused suffering and death. But they were matched by waves of people and money bringing help and healing." [2]

When speaking to the elders of Ephesus, Paul quoted Jesus as saying that it was more blessed to give than to receive (Acts 20:35). As a result, Paul worked hard as an apostle to provide for his own needs, the needs of his companions, and the poor. Elsewhere he admonishes thieves to find honest work and give to the poor (Eph 4:28). One motive for working hard, then, is to increase one's capacity to give.

As followers of Jesus we are stewards, or caretakers, of all the resources God has entrusted to us. We give in many ways. We share our time, our talent, and our treasure (or money). We give in response to the wonderful ways God has provided for our needs. We give to answer the psalmist's question: "What

can I offer the Lord for all he has done for me?" (Ps 116:12)
No gift could ever repay the Lord, but giving generously and
cheerfully in a variety of ways adds joy to Christian living. It
is indeed "blessed."

Journal

Jot a list of the ways you give in response to what the Lord
has done for you. What blessings have you experienced as a
steward or manager of God's resources? Is there a special gift
you might make to bolster the pastor–congregation partnership now forming in your church?

Day 22
"Holy Spirit"

Scripture Reading: Acts 2:1–21

Key Verse:

> *"I will pour out my Spirit upon all people."*
> —Acts 2:17

Pentecost was the birthday of the Church. What an exciting event! The wind and fire that day, described in Acts 2, were manifestations of the Holy Spirit, the third Person of the Trinity. Jesus told his followers that they would receive power when the Holy Spirit came on them (Acts 1:8). That promise was fulfilled on Pentecost. Once Jesus's followers had received the Holy Spirit, they were never the same again. Neither was our world.

The Holy Spirit dwells in each believer as a source of power, guidance, and encouragement. The Holy Spirit directs Christians and congregations as they carry out their service in the world. The Spirit brings unity and gives different kinds of spiritual gifts to believers for the purpose of building up the church. The Spirit confirms our identity as children of God.

The Holy Spirit is given as a pledge, a guarantee of our future home with God in heaven. The Spirit works within us to make us more and more like Christ. The result of this work is a cluster of wonderful qualities known as the fruit of the Spirit: "love, joy, peace, patience, kindness, goodness, faithfulness, gentleness, and self-control" (Gal 5:22–23).

As we grow up spiritually, no portion of our lives is left untouched by the Spirit. "If we are living now by the Holy

Spirit, let us follow the Holy Spirit's leading in every part of our lives" (Gal 5:25). The changes the Spirit makes in us unfold over time in a lifelong process leading to a glorious conclusion. "This promise is to you and to your children, and even to the Gentiles—all who have been called by the Lord our God" (Acts 2:39).

Journal

Do you sense that the Holy Spirit is active in your life? How? Do you sense that the Holy Spirit is active in the life of your congregation? Which fruits of the Spirit are evident in your life, and in the life of your church? Can you write a brief description of an event or story that illustrates the Spirit's ongoing work in your life, or the life of your church?

Day 23
"The Chain"

Scripture Reading: 2 Timothy 2:1–7

Key Verse:
> *"Teach these great truths to trustworthy people*
> *who are able to pass them on to others."*
> —2 Timothy 2:2

A man in Virginia Beach set a record by making the world's longest gum wrapper chain. He started it in 1965. Over the years he folded more than a million wrappers neatly into interlocking links. Now his creation is over eight miles long. It has won him a place in the record books.

Imagine that you are a link in a chain. You are connected to two other links, one up the chain from you, the other down the chain. Your strength, and the integrity of your connection to the other links, helps determine the strength of the entire chain. As the saying goes (and a popular TV game show reminded us), a chain is only as strong as its weakest link.

The Apostle Paul devoted his Christian life to making a chain. Paul's chain was not made of gum wrappers, however, it was made of people. Barnabas was known and well respected by believers in Jerusalem. He sponsored Paul and helped him win acceptance among the apostles (Acts 9:27). Paul, in turn, sponsored a young Christian leader named Timothy. Paul was so fond of Timothy that he referred to him as "my dear son" (2 Tm 2:1). That is a strong connection! Paul trained and encouraged Timothy so that he would become a strong link in the chain of Jesus's followers. Finally, Paul exhorted Timothy to add links of his own to the chain by teaching others what he had been taught. To whom should Timothy teach these things? "To trustworthy people who are able to pass them on to others" (2 Tm 2:2). Clearly, Paul anticipated that the links Timothy added would continue the process of adding new links.

They did. The chain of Jesus's followers continues to this very day, and you are an important part of it.

Journal

Write down some of the names of those who taught you the great truths of the Christian faith. Who showed you by example what it meant to live as a disciple of Jesus? Who are you now teaching? Who is learning about Christian living from your example?

Day 24
"Now What?"

Scripture Reading: Matthew 18:15–20

Key Verse:

> *"If another believer sins against you … "*
>
> —Matthew 18:15

Experts tell us that there are two kinds computer users: those who have lost data because of a system crash, and those who will. Use computers long enough, and you will eventually experience system failure and the problematic loss of data that follows in its wake.

It can also be said that there are two kinds of church members: those who have been sinned against by a fellow Christian, and those who will. We vary in our notions of what it means to be sinned against. Some Christians seem sensitive to the least provocation or personal slight. They continually feel sinned against. Others are more understanding and slow to take offense. Sooner or later, however, we all are sinned against.

Being sinned against by a fellow Christian pains us for at least two reasons. First, there is the personal pain. We trusted the person or expected certain things from him and now he has betrayed our trust or let us down. Second, there is our disappointment with the Church as the Body of Christ. We assumed that this kind of thing would not occur among members of a church, the family of God. We had hoped for more from a fellowship of believers. This loss of our ideal notions about Christians and churches compounds the personal pain we feel.

Jesus gave us clear instructions for a situation like this. When sinned against, we are to go directly to the one who sinned against us and speak with that person, one-on-one. If that effort is unsuccessful we are to return to the person, bringing along one or two others who serve as witnesses. If even this effort fails to produce a positive result, we are to take the matter to the Church, whose determination is binding.

Jesus's teaching on this topic is simple and practical. It is also widely ignored, which results in additional and unnecessary pain and misunderstanding. When you are sinned against, follow these steps.

Journal

Write the name of a Christian who has sinned against you. What steps have you taken in response? You can begin by going directly to the person to point out the fault, and proceed from there. Ask the Lord in prayer how to proceed. Then follow through.

Day 25
"Household"

Scripture Reading: 1 Timothy 3:1–5

Key Verse:
> *"An elder ... must manage his own family well ..."*
> —1 Timothy 3:4

The members of a pastor's family can feel blessed and oppressed at the same time. They may feel blessed because the fruits of obedience to God's call have provided them with a powerful sense of being in the center of God's will. There they enjoy a sense of security and well-being found nowhere else. They feel blessed to know many loving, supportive people in the Church. They often receive extraordinary kindness from people in the wider community as well. And they usually develop special kinship with the family members of other clergy.

These blessings are great. Mingled with them, however, are other factors that cause some clergy family members to feel oppressed. Boundaries between home and work become blurred. Privacy lessens. Demands are unrelenting. Some people may have unrealistic expectations for the pastor and members of the pastor's family. These and other aspects of clergy family life bring occasional feelings of frustration or resentment.

In some surveys, pastors have said that they believed that their calling to serve as pastors has affected family life negatively. Other pastors say that their calling has influenced family life for the better. The same pastors might respond differently to the question at different times in the family life cycle—or even at different times during the same week!

The Scriptures teach that a leader who fails to manage the household well is not qualified to take care of God's Church. No one has the right to expect perfection from any family, but this is good reason to support pastors, their spouses, and their children. Pray for them.

Journal

List the names of your pastor and all the members of the pastor's family. Linger prayerfully over each name, asking God to guide you in how to pray for that person. If appropriate, send a note of appreciation to one or more of them.

Day 26
"Be Encouraged"

Scripture Reading: Romans 1:8–12

Key Verse:

> *"I'm eager to encourage you in your faith,*
> *but I also want to be encouraged by yours."*
> —Romans 1:12

Scorching heat and scarce water make survival in the desert impossible for most animals. The hostile environment prevents many animals from living there. However, some animals have adapted to the harsh surroundings and discovered ways to thrive. Kangaroo rats, for example, manufacture water through body processes after eating dry seeds. They live in underground dens that they seal off to block out midday heat and recycle the moisture from their own breathing. These rodents do very well in the desert by getting the most from every particle of moisture.

Encouragement is like water in the desert. It is as essential to our spirits as moisture is to our bodies. Encouragement motivates us in our Christian service. Without it, our energy drains. We become listless and weak like a parched man languishing in an arid desert. When that man happens on an oasis, what rejoicing ensues! He chortles with delight and splashes about like a child frolicking in a sprinkler.

The apostle Paul wanted desperately to visit the Christians in Rome. He planned to bless them by offering encouragement. He expected that they would encourage his faith as well. Christians who meet to exchange encouragement in this way are like friends in the desert who share a long, cool, refreshing drink. It is interesting to note that Rome was famous for its elaborate system of aqueducts. These pipes and canals were a major engineering achievement. They brought water to Rome from as far away as fifty-seven miles. Some of them are still in use.

From time to time we all get thirsty for encouragement. We must be alert when it is offered and savor it the way kangaroo rats capture moisture in the desert. Then we can pour out some encouragement for others (Rom 12:8).

Journal

Write a list of the things that encourage you. Why are these meaningful? Now consider the needs of others. Plan to say or do something to encourage someone today.

Day 27
"Take Care"

Scripture reading: John 21:15–19

Key Verse:

> *"Jesus said, 'Take care of my sheep.'"*
>
> —John 21:16

After denying Jesus, Peter may have assumed that he could never again serve his Lord (Mt 26:69–75). What use could he possibly be? Yet Peter's hopes and usefulness were restored after the resurrection in a face-to-face exchange with Jesus (Jn 21:15–19). Jesus's three questions mirror Peter's three denials. Three times Peter affirms his love for Jesus, and three times Jesus replies by challenging Peter to feed or care for his sheep.

Pastors have found instruction in this exchange between Jesus and Peter. In it, they have discerned two important functions of pastoral leadership: Pastors are to love the Lord and feed his sheep.

Loving the Lord is the first responsibility of every pastor and indeed, every Christian (Mt 22:37). This love is expressed through obedience to Jesus (Jn 14:21) and love for one's neighbor (1 Jn 4:20).

Feeding the sheep involves preaching and teaching. Pastors share the word of God with their flocks. Paul exhorts Timothy, "Be a good worker, one who does not need to be ashamed and who correctly explains the word of truth" (2 Tm 2:15).

A pastor who loves Jesus and shares God's word with the congregation in clear and compelling fashion will serve a flock that is well-fed, cared for, and secure.

Journal

How does a pastor express his love for Jesus? List two or three specific ways. Next, write a brief description of good preaching. Why is the pastor's preaching ministry important?

Day 28
"Speak Up"

Scripture Reading: Ephesians 4:17-32

Key Verse:
> *"Don't let the sun go down while you are still angry,*
> *for anger gives a mighty foothold to the Devil."*
> —Ephesians 4:26-27

Anger is a natural emotion felt by everyone from time to time. It is extreme annoyance or displeasure. Bottled up, anger festers and grows. This can lead to an explosion in which people say and do destructive things they later regret. Channeled thoughtfully, however, anger can lead to good conversation.

The way Christians handle anger should set us apart from others who profess no belief in God. As new creations in Christ, we throw off the old sinful nature and display a new nature (Eph 4:22, 24). The action words, "throw off" and "display," relate to baptism rituals in the early church. Converts removed their old garments, symbolically casting off the old nature. Then they professed their faith in Jesus and passed through the waters of baptism. They emerged from the water to put on new white garments that represented the new nature in Christ.

Managing anger is a test of our ability to throw off the old nature and display the new. Christians speak up when they feel angry because being open and direct denies the enemy "a mighty foothold." It brings the tension to light so that those involved can resolve the problem.

Some people use the ABC approach when responding to anger. Ask, "What am I feeling and why?" Bring the concerns to God in prayer. Communicate your feelings in a positive manner. Ask, Bring, Communicate = ABC. The anger should be communicated soon—before the sun sets—so that it may be dispelled before it gives a foothold.

Journal

Write a description of the last time you felt angry. What led to those feelings? Bring them to God in prayer, and then communicate them in a clear, controlled manner.

Day 29
"Investing"

Scripture Reading: Romans 16:1–16

Key Verse:

> *"Greet each other in Christian love."*
>
> —Romans 16:16

In the first century, the letters of Paul were read aloud in the house churches. People were summoned by news that a letter had arrived. As they gathered to hear the letter, the air was charged with excitement. People listened intently as the epistle was read aloud to the entire assembly that very day. They savored the wisdom of one of God's choice servants.

When Paul concluded the letter with personal greetings, we can imagine smiles on the faces of those singled out for recognition. The final chapter of Romans is stuffed like a Christmas stocking with personal greetings. Paul mentions one name after another, and each one is tethered to a specific compliment or commendation. Some risked their lives for Paul, others were among the first converts to Christ in a certain territory, and still others had received Paul as kin. Clearly, Paul loved these people. Appreciation is the language of love.

Relationships are the lifeblood of healthy churches. People who care deeply for God and one another create fellowship. Even if he'd never met them personally, Paul wanted Christians to be encouraged and knit together in love by their ties to a fellowship of believers (Col 2:2).

How are strong bonds formed between people of faith? In Romans 16, Paul mentions those who have been his coworkers in the task of sharing the Good News. These people have shared adventures together. They have taken risks, endured hardships, made sacrifices, and helped one another in times of need. If they were all together in one room they would share stories, memories, laughter, and tears. They would discuss the joys and burdens known only to those who have left lesser things to follow Jesus together with undivided hearts.

Journal

Describe one or two experiences you have shared with others in your church that have produced strong bonds of fellowship. When your church members gather together, do you express appreciation for one another? Is your church providing enough opportunities for people to bond through shared service?

Day 30
"Bearing Fruit"

Scripture Reading: John 15:1–8

Key Verse:

> *"My true disciples produce much fruit."*
>
> —John 15:8

On a chilly autumn evening, a bonfire is magnetic. Its orange glow draws people eager to warm themselves while gazing on the mesmerizing flicker of its flames. Those crackling flames roast hotdogs and marshmallows and create thirst quenched by cups of cider. A bonfire also leaves a distinctive lingering impression: The scent of smoke remains with jackets and sweatshirts for days.

Jesus once created the image of a bonfire in the minds of his listeners when he taught them about discipleship. He compared unproductive disciples to kindling. Branches that bear no fruit are gathered into a pile to be burned. Anyone who separates from Jesus soon becomes as withered and barren as a branch severed from the vine. Apart from him, we are spiritually impotent. Our potential for promoting the reign of God goes up in smoke.

If we remain in Jesus and his words remain in us, the results are dramatically different. Instead of kindling waiting for the match, we are sturdy vines laden with ripe, juicy fruit. Our Heavenly Father, like a master gardener, will prune us for even greater fruitfulness. Our connection with Jesus gives us life and produces results in our service for him.

The fruit of a disciple is another disciple (Mt 28:19). When followers of Jesus produce other disciples who produce still more, fruitfulness abounds. This, Jesus said, "brings great glory to my Father." More than bonfires, gardeners love harvests.

Journal

Sketch yourself as a branch, Jesus as the vine, and the skilled hand of the master gardener, our Heavenly Father. How strong or tenuous is the link between branch and vine? Do you stay with Jesus, and do his words remain in you? How? What additional pruning might lead to even greater fruitfulness?

Dialogue Meeting 3

This is the third of four dialogue meetings in the *Welcome, Pastor!* process. You are developing relationships of love and trust with fellow participants. Before, you may have been unwilling to risk sharing some things with them. Now, however, you are ready to speak openly and honestly. Fruit from this process of prayer and dialogue is ripening! Those who prevail will harvest it. *"So, my dear brothers and sisters, be strong and steady, always enthusiastic about the Lord's work, for you know that nothing you do for the Lord is ever useless"* (1 Cor 15:58). Listen lovingly during this dialogue meeting. Seek to understand the thoughts and feelings expressed by others. Do you hear themes emerging?

Dialogue Starters

1. Have you sensed that God has spoken to you in the past ten days? If so, in what way(s)?

2. What are you learning about the pastor–people partnership that is currently under construction?

3. What ideas or insights from your devotional time during the past ten days seem especially meaningful to you?

4. Are the daily journaling exercises helpful?

5. Finish this sentence: "For me, this ten-day period of devotions has been like … ."

6. How would you like the group to pray for you during the next ten days? Be specific.

By the end of this meeting, members of your congregation are well acquainted with the new pastor. The new pastor is learning how to care for and lead the people of the church. A partnership is forming. This partnership is one-of-a-kind, because every pastor-congregation pairing is unique. Prayer is shaping this venture in ways that will allow both pastor and congregation to thrive, to the glory of God. Only ten days remain. Press on!

Day 31
"Unity"

Scripture Reading: Ephesians 4:1-6

Key Verse:
> *"Always keep yourselves united in the Holy Spirit,*
> *and bind yourselves together with peace."*
> —Ephesians 4:3

Unity is rare. It becomes threatened, sooner or later, whenever two or more people begin a cooperative venture. Unless the people involved prize unity and are willing to labor for it, it will wane. Marriages end in divorce. Task groups in the workplace are rent by conflict and become unproductive. Competing visions paralyze community service organizations. Lack of unity stalls progress.

The church is not exempt from these consequences. In fact, disunity is nearly as old as the church itself (*see* 1 Cor 1:10). When churches fragment into factions, all pay a dear price. Feelings are hurt, misunderstandings multiply, and progress on kingdom goals is stymied. The wider community forfeits the positive impact that a united church would have generated. Cynics gather more ammunition for their bulging arsenals of evidence that Christians fail to walk their talk.

The Scriptures warn us to guard our unity. Called by God, we are to be humble and gentle. We are to be patient and make allowances for one another's faults because of our love. We are to bind ourselves together with peace. The Holy Spirit is the source of our unity. So the Apostle Paul wrote to the Corinthians: "Some of us are Jews, some are Gentiles, some are slaves, and some are free. But we have all been baptized into Christ's body by one Spirit, and we have all received the same Spirit" (1 Cor 12:13).

Unity is God's gift to us in Christ (Eph 2:18). Jesus has already done what was needed to break down dividing walls of hostility. When we adopt the attitudes and behaviors that promote unity, we claim this precious gift and show that we understand its enormous value.

Journal

Reread the list of qualities that promote unity. Which of those traits describe you? Which one would you like to pursue more intentionally? Write a prayer asking for God's help in that endeavor.

Day 32
"Honesty"

Scripture Reading: John 1:35–50

Key Verse:
> *"Here comes an honest man—a true son of Israel."*
> —John 1:47

Jesus knew the thoughts (Mk 8:17) and motives (Mt 22:18) of the people around him. His powers of perception enabled him to assess the character of a man very quickly. This insight proved invaluable as he met and called the men who would become his followers. As Nathanael approached, Jesus declared him "an honest man" (Jn 1:47). The statement rang true in Nathanael's ears. He was so impressed that he became a disciple of Jesus despite the fact that he wondered at first whether anybody worth meeting could possibly be from Nazareth (Jn 1:46).

Honesty, in the sense used to describe Nathanael, means more than simply being truthful, just, or fair. It means having no pretensions. With Nathanael, what you saw was what you got. He was the same person with all people and in every situation. He never put on airs or tried to act like someone he wasn't. Nathanael was open and transparent.

Those of us who fear rejection consider this kind of honesty risky. We want as many people as possible to accept us and, preferably, to like us. As a result, we try to read others' expectations of us and act accordingly. Like the chameleon whose color changes in different environments, we appear differently in different settings. Managing impressions in this way may not be intentionally deceptive, but it is less than honest because it can be misleading.

When we realize at the core of our being that God knows all about us, yet accepts us as we are and loves us without condition, our lives change. We no longer depend on others to validate or accept us. We can be honest, transparent, and unpretentious. We will expect others to be open, too. Honesty truly is the best policy.

Journal

If you have recently been tempted to manage the impression you were making on another person, jot down a quick description of the occasion. What motivated you? How might you have behaved in a more genuine manner? What specific thing might you do to encourage others to be transparent with you? Write a prayer of thanks for God's unconditional love.

Day 33
"What's In a Name?"

Scripture Reading: Matthew 1:18–25

Key Verse:
> *"And she will have a son, and you are to name him Jesus,*
> *for he will save his people from their sins."*
> —Matthew 1:21

When parents name their children, they do something very important. A name is typically with that person from the cradle to the grave. It is the world's signpost to the person's identity.

Joseph's decision to name Jesus was important because, by naming this child, Joseph declared that the baby belonged to the house of David. Prophets had foretold that the Messiah would come from the house and lineage of David (Is 11:1). Because Joseph was of David's line, any child Joseph named was, too. In obedience to God, Joseph named the child Jesus, meaning "God saves." As Jesus himself put it years later, he came not to be served but to serve, to give his life a ransom for many (Mk 10:45). And he encouraged us to offer our petitions in his name (Jn 14:13–14).

How did you get your name? What reasons have your parents given for choosing it for you? Do you have a namesake? If so, have you met that person? What qualities does or did that person possess?

Surnames are also important. They connect generations. Some families teach children that the family name is meaningful, that it stands for important values. Sometimes symbols

representing these values are embossed on a family crest. Up-
holding them is the responsibility of each new generation of
family members.

Church names can shape the identity of congregations. The founding members of some churches base the
name of their congregation on geography. Others choose a
biblical name, or a name describing what the church offers to
nonmembers. Do you know how your congregation got its
name?

Journal

Sketch a crest depicting the most important values to you,
your extended family, or your congregation. How do these
values shape your behavior?

Day 34
"A Song of Praise"

Scripture Reading: Psalm 107

Key Verse:
> *"Those who are wise will take all this to heart;*
> *they will see in our history the faithful love of the LORD."*
> —Psalm 107:43

God's character and competence were uppermost in the minds of those who wrote the Book of Psalms, the hymnbook of Israel. The Lord is so wonderful that he is to be praised in the morning and the evening, the daytime and the nighttime, by everything that lives (Ps 150:6). He is to be praised forever (Ps 5:11).

Psalms are hymns that inspire, and they are also teaching tools. For years before they were collected in written form, the psalms were performed and sung in public worship. Psalms such as 107 are salvation history psalms. They rehearse the mighty acts of God in many times and places. They retell epic tales of rescue and redemption. These psalms teach worshipers the story of God's people. They demonstrate the Lord's faithful love to those who ponder God's mighty acts in history.

Considering God's actions in the past is not merely an academic exercise. We remember God's force in history because he commands us to do so (Is 46:9). We remember because it bolsters our faith. Salvation history psalms inspire us to trust God in the present by reminding us of his faithfulness in the past.

If you were to write a personal salvation history psalm, what events would you include? If your congregation were to write a song praising God for God's faithfulness through your history, what occasions and experiences would comprise the lyrics?

Journal

Make a list of God's mighty acts in your personal life or throughout the history of your congregation. Then write a salvation history psalm similar in form to Psalm 107.

Day 35
"Seeking"

Scripture Reading: Luke 19:1–10

Key Verse:
> *"And I, the Son of Man, have come to seek and save
> those like him who are lost."*
>   —Luke 19:10

Zacchaeus had very few friends. He was a tax collector who had become very wealthy, but he was scorned by his fellow Jews in Jericho. They despised him for collecting taxes on behalf of the Roman occupiers of Palestine. Zacchaeus was a social outcast, and no amount of money could fully compensate for the sting of public rejection.

Passing through Jericho, Jesus looked up into the sycamore tree and called Zacchaeus down from his perch. He walked home with Zacchaeus and ate a delicious meal with him. Onlookers were scandalized. How could a holy man sit at table with a notorious sinner?

Jesus risked misunderstanding and ridicule to reach out to needy people. This was why he had come, he said: to seek and to save those who are lost.

Christians must share our Lord's passion for reaching the lost—those who do not yet know Jesus Christ and his love for them. We search out people on the margins and we look for those on the outside of the church looking in. We build relationships with the ones who imagine that they would never be accepted if they visited a church. We do not wait for them to come to church; we go to them. We enter their homes, and

we invite them into ours. We share life with them. As we so-
cialize with unchurched people, we win their trust, listening
carefully as they open their hearts and minds to us. And when
the time is right, we invite them into the family of God. This
family is not composed of deserving people. To the contrary,
every one of us is a debtor to grace. Jesus taught the crowd
in Jericho that day that no person or group is outside the
bounds of God's redeeming love. Aren't you glad?

Journal

Are you aware of a person or group who may feel excluded
from the family of God? Write their names in your journal.
If anything were possible, how would you reach out to that
person or group? Does your congregation take advantage
of opportunities to reach out to unchurched people in your
community? List the ways you already do this. If that list is
short, read your local newspaper while asking God to show
you a need to which you could respond.

Day 36
"Forgiven!"

Scripture Reading: Matthew 18:21–35

Key Verse:
> *"Shouldn't you have mercy on your fellow servant,*
> *just as I had mercy on you?"*
> —Matthew 18:33

Ink. Lipstick. Chocolate. Grass. Grease. These words strike fear into the hearts of anyone who does laundry. Stains ruin clothes. And they have created an industry of cleaning supplies and spot removers, all promising to restore the luster of soiled garments.

Scripture compares our sin to a stain (Ps 51:1, 9). We are a fallen people. Our transgressions are a blot upon us, marring God's image in us and soiling God's good intentions. We may deeply regret our sin and fervently wish that the stain could be taken away. But we cannot remove this stain ourselves, no matter how we try. Only God can do that.

Thanks to God, Jesus made atonement for our sins on the cross of Calvary (1 Pt 3:18). His sacrifice cleansed us from the stain of sin (Heb 1:3). Now we can confess our sins and receive God's forgiveness, cleansing, and restoration. "Oh, what joy for those whose rebellion is forgiven, whose sin is put out of sight!" (Ps 32:1) When we receive the grace of God, our sins wash away. They are removed from us as far as the east is from the west (Ps 103:12).

In the story of the unforgiving debtor, Jesus directs an intense spotlight on a widespread form of ingratitude. A person forgiven a huge debt refuses to offer pardon to someone owing him far less. We can see ourselves in this story. How easy it is to receive God's grace and then deny grace to others. Someone once observed that we commonly think that forgiveness is a wonderful idea until we have something to forgive. When we have something to forgive, we can be sure that it will not be easy for us. We are too proud, too self-absorbed to pardon others without a struggle. It helps to remember that we are ourselves pardoned debtors.

Journal

Imagine your sins were stains on a beautiful, priceless garment. Now see those stains removed by God's grace. Is there a grudge you should release in light of God's pardon for your sin?

Day 37
"Pain with a Purpose"

Scripture Reading: Acts 7:54–8:1, 11:19–20

Key Verse:

"A great wave of persecution began that day, sweeping over the church in Jerusalem, and all the believers except the apostles fled into Judea and Samaria."

—Acts 8:1

Like a handful of BBs dropped on a concrete floor, the believers in Jerusalem scattered after Stephen's martyrdom. They took off in all directions to avoid persecution. They traveled to places like Phoenicia, Cyprus, and Antioch of Syria. Everywhere they went, they shared the Good News about Jesus—but only with Jews. The evangelistic outreach of the early church was limited to Jewish people at first. But the events set in motion by Stephen's untimely death changed that.

" … some of the believers who went to Antioch from Cyprus and Cyrene began preaching to Gentiles about the Lord Jesus. The power of the Lord was upon them, and large numbers of these Gentiles believed and turned to the Lord" (Acts 11:20–21). This is a remarkable turn of events! Jewish Christians first began to reach out to Gentiles in the wake of persecution sparked by the murder of Stephen. The Christian movement widened its scope. It became a global phenomenon. Tertullian, a church leader who lived in the second century, saw so many developments like this that he declared, "The blood of the martyrs is the seed of the church."

The death of Stephen was a shattering blow to the early church. It was painful. But as the Book of Acts unfolds, we see the purpose: God worked through the death of Stephen and the ensuing persecution to get the gospel to the Gentiles.

Hardship and tragedy come to us unbidden. They wreak havoc upon us, disrupting our lives and spoiling our plans. But God often works through tragedy to manifest blessings. When we must endure pain, let us seek God's purpose. We may be privileged to identify the blessings, or we may not. It is, finally, a matter of trust.

Journal

Write about a time in your life when a tragedy furthered God's purpose. Can you also identify pain with a purpose in the history of your congregation?

Day 38
"Integrity"

Scripture Reading: Titus 2:1–8

Key Verse:

"But as for you, promote the kind of living
that reflects right teaching."

—Titus 2:1

Titus was a teacher. People gathered to hear his lessons. The content of these lessons was Christian doctrine. Titus taught that the grace of God for all people had been revealed in Jesus Christ. In a sinful world, some rejected his message. Despite this, Titus persisted, passing on to others the truth he himself had received. His was a great responsibility.

Titus had a mentor named Paul. Paul described his calling in the first verse of this letter: "I have been sent to bring faith to those God has chosen and to teach them to know the truth that shows them how to live godly lives" (Ti 1:1). Here Paul is clear about the results of good instruction. Christian teaching transforms lives. It follows that Christian teachers live with integrity. Their words and actions line up. They walk the talk. They are able to do this because they know the truth that reveals how one may live right.

When a Christian teacher suffers a lapse of integrity, the witness of the entire church is compromised. The teacher suffers loss of reputation, obviously. But this is only the first domino in a chain reaction of adverse consequences. The teacher's students are discouraged. Christians in the wider congregation are saddened, and non-Christian onlookers surmise that truth revealing how to live a godly life doesn't exist or must be sought elsewhere.

Serving as a teacher in the church is a serious matter (Jas 3:1). We who respond to this high calling have set our hearts on something precious. If we bear in mind the importance of integrity, we will not need to lose it before appreciating its value. No one is perfect, but we cannot sidestep the crucial impact of the example we set (Ti 2:7).

Journal

Have you had the privilege of being instructed by a Christian teacher who set an example for you? Write the name of that teacher and a list of his or her qualities. Is there anyone who looks to you as a teacher, formally or informally? How important is it to you to adhere consistently to high moral principles?

Day 39
"Lead On"

Scripture Reading: Romans 12:1–8

Key Verse:

> *"If God has given you leadership ability,*
> *take the responsibility seriously."*

—Romans 12:8

God has gifted certain Christians with the ability to lead. The roles they fill may be formal or informal. A formal leader may have a title with a job description and term of office, while an informal leader may have none of those things. All leaders make an essential contribution to the congregation as it fulfills God's call.

When we serve in a leadership position, we may feel inadequate. We may believe that we lack the background, training, and spiritual maturity to fulfill our role. These feelings are common among those called to serve God. Moses, Isaiah, and Paul all protested when summoned to lead. They were concerned about their limitations: Moses was not a good speaker (Ex 4:10), Isaiah was a sinful man (Is 6:5), and Paul had persecuted the Church (1 Cor 15:9). Yet God used each of these leaders in wonderful ways despite their faults.

When Paul addressed the Church in Rome about the gifts each Christian has been given for service, he mentioned leadership specifically. He did not demand perfection from leaders. He knew from his own experience that a Christian leader's weaknesses could be the very things God used to accomplish wonderful things (2 Cor 12:10). So instead of insisting on flawlessness, Paul asked only that persons gifted for leadership take their responsibility seriously.

Christians serious about leadership become committed servants. Jesus is our role model for servant leadership. When his disciples bickered over who was most prominent and important, Jesus offered them a new way of thinking about significance and greatness (Mt 20:20-28). If we have the hearts of servants, we will take our leadership responsibility seriously. We will love Christ and others too much to let them down.

Journal

Complete this sentence: "A Christian leader is someone who … ." List the specific behaviors that demonstrate that a church leader takes the responsibility seriously.

Day 40
"What Endures"

Scripture Reading: 1 Corinthians 13:1–13

Key Verse:
*"There are three things that will endure—faith, hope, and love—
and the greatest of these is love."*
—1 Corinthians 13:13

We have reached the end of our 40-day journey. We have searched the Scriptures for insight on the four key challenges to successful start up:

1. **Getting to know one another** by sharing love and laughter, hurts and hopes
2. **Sharing faith** honestly and authentically
3. **Discerning what God expects** of us as pastor and people
4. **Speaking openly about differences** in order to handle them constructively

We have engaged in dialogue about things God is teaching us through Bible reading, meditation, and one another. What remains to be said about building a healthy, enduring, and productive pastor–congregation partnership?

Pastors and congregations whose partnership produces great results are bound together in love. Their partnership may not lead to fame or public recognition. Their results may not be considered great as the world measures greatness, but the love between them works miracles. They resolve conflicts, confess sins, receive forgiveness, reach out to the lost, and

serve others for the common good. Their love deepens over
the years. Their lives are knit together in a breathtaking tapestry of memory composed of smiles and tears, celebrations
and sorrows.

The love between a pastor and congregation endures
because it is eternal. It "never gives up, never loses faith, is
always hopeful, and endures through every circumstance"
(1 Cor 13:7). It is the love of God.

Journal

Sketch a tapestry illustrating the ways God knits together
the lives of Christians through shared experience over time.
Write briefly about the enduring legacy you want to result
from your pastor-congregation partnership.

Dialogue Meeting 4

"Well done, good servant!" (Lk 19:17) Congratulations on completing forty days of prayer and journaling. Make this final dialogue meeting a celebration. You may wish to share a meal or exchange simple gifts to commemorate your time together on this 40-day journey. Through prayer and dialogue you have built a productive pastor–congregation partnership. You have gotten to know one another by sharing love and laughter, hurts and hopes. You have shared faith honestly and authentically. You have discerned what God expects of you as pastor and people. And you have spoken openly about differences in order to handle them constructively. At this dialogue meeting, allow plenty of time for everyone to participate. Invite quieter members to address the group if they wish to do so.

Dialogue Starters

1. Have you sensed that God has spoken to you in the past ten days? If so, in what way(s)?

2. What have you learned about pastor–congregation partnership through this process?

3. What would you like to learn more about?

4. What ideas or insights from your devotional time during the past forty days seem especially meaningful to you now?

5. How would you finish this sentence? "For me, this forty-day period of devotions has been like … ."

6. Are you aware of any unfinished business related to pastoral start-up? If so, how do you think it might be addressed?

7. Conclude the sharing in your group by inviting each person to complete this sentence: "I thank God for … ."

You have invested the time and energy required to seek God's help in building a strong pastor–congregation partnership. The process is drawing to a close, but the partnership is only beginning. You've built the foundation of a lighthouse. In days to come you will add the tower and light the beacon. Jesus said, "*You are the light of the world—like a city on a mountain, glowing in the night for all to see. Don't hide your light under a basket! Instead, put it on a stand and let it shine for all*" (Mt 5:14-15).

When a pastor and a congregation build a strong partnership, they serve together in harmony for many years. They appreciate each other deeply, handle differences in a constructive manner, and make allowances for one another's weaknesses. They love each other with the love of Christ. The light of their love shines. "*Let your good deeds shine out for all to see,*" Jesus said, "*so that everyone will praise your heavenly Father*" (Mt 5:17).

ABOUT DIALOGUE MEETINGS

Dialogue? "Can't we just talk about it?" Talk is important, but it's only half of dialogue. Equally important is the other half: *listening*. Dialogue meetings allow you to share and celebrate God's work among you as you build the foundation of a new partnership.

Schedule four dialogue meetings in advance; one each after Day 10, Day 20, Day 30, and Day 40. Let everyone know times and locations, and invite them to bring their journals. Assign a leader for each meeting. This duty can rotate among several people. Begin and end on time. Hold these meetings in a quiet, comfortable space free of distractions and interruptions. Turn off cell phones. Make the space as hospitable as possible. Offer light refreshments. Use name tags. Greet people warmly as they arrive, and seat them in circles of eight.

At the appointed start time, welcome everyone and thank them for coming. Ask them to silently read "The Art and Practice of Dialogue" in the Appendix. Next, read aloud Psalm 85:8–9 or another Scripture passage of your choosing and invite the group to observe three full minutes of silence. Signal the end of the silence and invite persons to speak when they wish. Use Dialogue Starters to focus the speaking and listening.

APPENDIX:
THE ART AND PRACTICE OF DIALOGUE

"The wise person makes learning a joy."
—Proverbs 15:2

Dialogue is different from everyday conversation. Instead of speaking carelessly, we begin by observing silence. The silence invites our own deepest knowing and creates space for wisdom to emerge.

Dialogue is an art. To learn this art, be open and empty. Adopt a beginner's mind. Ask questions. Listen carefully. Allow others to be your teachers. Be thankful for them. Welcome creativity.

Explore dialogue like this:

- Sit in a circle

- Stop talking. Take a vow of silence. Speak only to improve on the silence and to be in service of meaning and community.

- Openness is the rule, not the exception.

- Listen to understand.

- Notice your assumptions and inner voice.

- Imagine the other person's perspective.

- Explore the other's intentions and assumptions by asking questions like, "Do you mean…" and "What is your understanding of … ."

- Allow others to see your perspective and your assumptions.

- Use a 'talking stick,' or another symbol to pass from one person to another. Only the one holding the symbol is recognized as the speaker.

- Question from a place of genuine not knowing.

- Seek and serve Christ in others.

- Don't wait for silence before speaking. Wait for the silence to end.

(To learn more about dialogue, explore the work of William Isaacs and David Bohm.)

END NOTES/BIBLIOGRAPHY

Introduction

[1] *A New Beginning for Pastors and Congregations,* Jossey-Bass, 1999, p. 7

Day 21

[2] Source: Volunteer relief worker in Phuket, Thailand interviewed by Dan Rather on CBS Evening News, January 5, 2005.

ABOUT THE AUTHOR

Fredrick B. Oaks has served as a pastor since 1983. He also provides information and encouragement to pastors and lay people partnering with God for renewal in older churches through "Church Over 40." (See www.ChurchOver40.com.) Fred holds a Bachelor of Arts degree in Social Work from Augustana College in Rock Island, Illinois and a Master of Divinity degree with honors from the Northern Baptist Theological Seminary of Chicago. Fred and his wife Judy have three children: Aaron, Emily, and Allison Joy.

Welcome, Pastor! is available in bulk quantities for group study. For order and pricing information consult the publisher's website (www.faithwalkpub.com) or call 800-335-7177.

10 copies	1-932902-00-7
25 copies	1-932902-01-5
100 copies	1-932902-02-3